Mortgage Chronicles

THE UNTOLD FACTS

GREGORY WARD

Copyright

© 2025 Gregory Ward. All rights reserved.

No part of this publication may be reproduced, stored in a retrieval system, or transmitted in any form or by any means (electronic, mechanical, photocopying, recording, or otherwise) without the prior written permission of the publisher, except for brief quotations used in reviews or articles.

This book is inspired by the author's personal experiences in mortgage financing. It is written for informational purposes only and does not serve as financial or legal advice.

Readers should consult professionals for guidance related to their specific circumstances. The author and publisher assume no responsibility for errors, omissions, or different outcomes resulting from the use of the information provided.

If you would like to reach the Author, contact him at: gregdw@sbcglobal.net

Foreword

Homeownership has long been viewed as a cornerstone of financial stability and personal achievement in the United States. Yet for many, the path to the front door can feel confusing and uncertain. The mortgage process involves important choices, careful planning and guidance that is clear and trustworthy. Too often, people move through it without the understanding or confidence they deserve.

This book serves an important purpose. It brings transparency to the lending process and bridges the gap between expectation and reality. It explains the steps in everyday language and shows why preparation, patience and responsible decision-making matter. It highlights the value of clarity, ethical guidance and steady communication between borrowers and loan officers.

The strength of this work lies in its simplicity and honesty. It does not rush the reader. Instead, it offers a clear path, practical insight and thoughtful encouragement. For first time homebuyers, it provides a calm foundation and answers questions that are often left unspoken. For mortgage professionals, it reinforces the importance of service, integrity and long-term client care.

Whether you are beginning your journey toward buying a home or supporting others through theirs, you will find helpful direction here. The principles in these pages reflect what makes lending meaningful: people, purpose and preparation.

Homeownership is more than a transaction. It is a milestone filled with hope, responsibility and opportunity. This guide honors that truth and supports it with knowledge and clarity.

Content

Introduction	1
Chapter 1	3
The Mortgage Reality—Opportunities and Traps	
Chapter 2	13
Understanding How Mortgages Work	
Chapter 3	18
How Mortgage Payments Are Calculated	
Chapter 4	24
The Credit Connection	
Chapter 5	34
Preparing for Pre-Approval	
Chapter 6	42
How To Choose the Right Mortgage	
Chapter 7	48
Shopping for a Lender, Not Just a Loan	
Chapter 8	56
The Loan Process Step by Step	
Chapter 9	63
Common Mortgage Mistakes and How to Avoid Them	
Chapter 10	70
The Emotional Side of Homebuying	
Chapter 11	76
The Loan Officer's Challenges	

Chapter 12	82
Life After the Loan	
Chapter 13	89
Building Financial Wisdom	
Chapter 14	95
The Future of Mortgage Lending	
Chapter 15	101
Final Reflections — More Than a Loan	
Conclusion	104
Bonus Resources	106
Communication Templates for Loan Officers	108
First-Time Homebuyer Program and Grant List in the United States	110
Glossary of Mortgage Terms	112
References	114

Introduction

Buying a home is one of the most important decisions many people make in their lifetime. It represents stability, personal growth and financial responsibility. Yet the mortgage process can feel complex, overwhelming and uncertain without the right guidance. Many borrowers step into this journey with excitement but little preparation, and confusion can quickly replace confidence if key steps are misunderstood.

It is easy to believe that lending is just paperwork and signatures. Over time, it becomes clear that each loan represents a family, a dream, and a set of financial realities. Over the years, I have learned that borrowers do not just need a loan; They need clarity, reassurance, and honest information.

I have also discovered that no two borrowers are the same. One client may have strong income but inconsistent credit habits. Another may have excellent credit but limited savings. Every situation requires patience, review, and a commitment to guiding the client with integrity. These lessons shaped the way I approach this profession and reinforced the importance of proper education in mortgage lending.

This book is designed to bring clarity to the mortgage experience. It is written for first time homebuyers who want to understand the process, and for loan officers who are committed to serving their clients with integrity and purpose. The information here outlines the steps, the expectations and the realities of mortgage lending in a clear and practical way.

Through this guide, readers will learn how mortgage programs work, how to avoid common mistakes and how to prepare for long-term homeownership. Loan officers will find guidance on communication, ethics and building lasting relationships in a competitive and evolving industry.

This book explains the mortgage process in a simple and useful way, supported by real experience and practices used every day lending environment. By the time you finish this book, you will understand the major loan programs, the role of credit, how underwriting works, what lenders expect and how to prepare for a smooth closing.

Homeownership is more than signing documents and receiving keys. It is a commitment to financial stability and future growth. When buyers understand the process and loan officers work with care, the mortgage journey becomes easier, smoother and more rewarding.

Chapter 1

The Mortgage Reality—Opportunities and Traps

Owning a home has always been an important part of the American dream. It gives families a sense of belonging, stability, and progress. For many people, buying a home is more than a financial step. It is a sign of independence and a way to build a lasting foundation for the future.

Yet the same opportunity that brings freedom can also create financial stress when misunderstood. Mortgages make homeownership possible, but they also require discipline and knowledge. The same loan that helps one family build equity can leave another struggling if they are not prepared for the full responsibility that comes with it.

A mortgage can be a powerful tool when used wisely. It allows people to buy homes they could not pay for outright, build credit, and grow long term wealth. It also keeps housing markets active and strengthens local communities.

But when handled without proper understanding, it can lead to serious financial problems.

Some borrowers focus only on getting approved for the largest amount possible instead of what they can comfortably afford. Others overlook property taxes, homeowners' insurance, maintenance costs, and other hidden expenses that come with owning a home.

The opportunity is in ownership.
The trap is in rushing, guessing, or taking advice from the wrong places.

How Misinformation, Poor Decisions, and Hidden Costs Keep Buyers Stuck

Information is everywhere, but not all of it is accurate. Borrowers often receive advice from well-meaning friends, social media, or outdated sources. Making decisions based on mixed guidance can lead to trouble.

A buyer who focuses only on the monthly payment and ignores closing costs may struggle at closing. Another may compare themselves to others and try to buy too much house, stretching their finances too thin.

Hidden costs can surprise buyers who are not prepared for property taxes, homeowners insurance, or private mortgage insurance.

When buyers do not fully understand the process, they can delay homeownership or make choices that strain their finances.

Success in getting a mortgage depends on planning, budgeting, and a clear understanding of how each decision affects the long-term picture.

Common Mortgage Misconceptions

Below are common misconceptions about mortgage lending:

1. *You must have perfect credit to buy a home.* Many believe they need flawless credit to qualify. In reality, several loan programs allow flexible credit standards. What matters most is consistent payment history, manageable debt, and willingness to improve. A loan officer can guide buyers on small steps that strengthen credit before applying.

2. *You must have a 20 percent down payment.* While a 20 percent down payment helps avoid private mortgage insurance, it is not required for most loans. FHA, VA, and USDA programs offer low or no down payment options. Many conventional lenders also accept smaller percentages depending on the borrower's profile.

3. *All lenders offer the same loan terms.* Lenders structure loans differently. Interest rates, fees, and service levels vary.

Comparing lenders helps borrowers find not only better rates but also better support and transparency.

4. *Pre-approval means guaranteed approval.*
Pre-approval is an important step, but it is not final approval. Any major change in credit, income, or debt before closing can affect the outcome. Borrowers should avoid new credit inquiries or large purchases after pre approval.

5. *Interest rates are the only thing that matters.*
A low rate may look attractive, but it does not always mean a better loan. Fees, points, and closing costs can make one offer more expensive than another. The best choice comes from comparing total loan cost, not just the rate.

6. *Renting is always cheaper than buying.*
Renting can seem easier, but it often builds no equity. In many areas, monthly rent is as high or higher than a mortgage payment. The difference is that a mortgage gradually builds ownership, while rent ends when you move out.

7. *Pre-qualification and pre-approval mean the same thing.*
Pre-qualification gives a rough estimate based on unverified information. Pre-approval involves reviewing documents and verifying income and credit. Sellers take pre approval more seriously because it shows real financial readiness.

8. *Once the loan closes, the process is over.*
   Homeownership continues after closing. Borrowers must stay on top of payments, escrow changes, and property taxes. The lender may sell or transfer servicing, but the borrower's responsibility remains.

9. *Home values always rise.*
   Home prices often increase over time, but markets move in cycles. Economic changes, job markets, and local factors can affect property values. Buyers should focus on long term stability, not short-term trends.

Common Challenges with Mortgage Loans

Appraisal Gaps and Low Valuations:

A common surprise for homebuyers is when the home appraisal comes in lower than the purchase price. This is called an appraisal gap. It happens when the price agreed upon is higher than what the appraiser determines the home is worth based on recent sales.

For example, if a buyer agrees to pay $400,000 for a home but the appraisal comes in at $380,000, the lender will base the loan on the lower amount. The buyer must then cover the difference out of pocket or renegotiate the price.

This can create stress and sometimes delay the deal. Buyers should plan for this possibility, especially in competitive markets where prices move quickly. A calm discussion with the loan officer and real estate agent can lead to solutions such as:

- Renegotiating with the seller
- Meeting halfway on the difference
- Using appraisal gap coverage if available
- Reviewing the comparable sales used in the report

Understanding that appraisals are a form of risk protection, not punishment, helps buyers stay realistic and prepared.

Underestimating Closing Costs:

Another issue that catches buyers off guard is closing costs. Many assume the down payment is the only major upfront expense, but closing costs can total between three and six percent of the home price.

These include lender fees, appraisal fees, title insurance, prepaid taxes, and homeowners' insurance. Some buyers are surprised when they learn they need more money at closing than expected.

The solution is simple. Always ask for a Loan Estimate early in the process.

This document lists every expected fee and gives a clear picture of total cash needed to close. Having this conversation early prevents last minute surprises and allows better budgeting.

Property Condition and Repair Requirements:

Many first-time buyers overlook property condition. Some loan programs, such as FHA or VA, require that homes meet certain safety and habitability standards before closing.

If an appraiser or inspector notes peeling paint, old wiring, or roof damage, the lender may delay or deny the loan until repairs are made. Sometimes sellers will not agree to make these fixes, leaving buyers to negotiate or walk away.

Knowing this early helps buyers set realistic expectations, especially when purchasing older homes. It is smart to discuss loan specific property standards with your loan officer before making an offer.

How the Economy Shapes Mortgage Reality

The housing market moves with the economy. When interest rates fall, more people qualify for loans and competition for homes rises. When rates increase, buying power drops and markets slow down.

Inflation, job growth, and government policies all affect what buyers experience. Understanding these trends helps borrowers plan better and make decisions that fit their goals. The best time to buy is when your finances are ready, not just when rates are low.

The Danger of Predatory Lending

Not every lender operates with the borrower's best interest in mind. Some take advantage of those who are uninformed or in a hurry to buy. Predatory practices such as inflated fees, hidden terms, or pressure tactics can cause lasting harm.

Buyers should read every document, ask questions, and choose lenders who explain clearly. A good loan officer focuses on long term success, not just closing a deal.

The Emotional Side of Borrowing

Buying a home is both financial and emotional. It represents hope, family, and a better future. That excitement can make people ignore warning signs. They may stretch their budget, overlook issues, or rush decisions out of fear of missing out.

A wise buyer keeps emotions in check and makes choices based on numbers and long-term comfort, not comparison.

The best loan officers help clients balance logic with emotion so they can make decisions they will not regret.

Technology and Information Overload

Online lenders and instant pre-approvals have made access to mortgages easier but not always clearer. A calculator can show a number, but it cannot tell you whether a loan truly fits your situation.

Technology is helpful when used with proper guidance. The best results come from combining digital tools with professional advice. Numbers are important, but context gives them meaning.

Developing the Right Mindset

A mortgage should be seen as a long-term partnership, not a quick deal. It requires patience, planning, and consistency. Borrowers who understand their income, debts, and goals make better choices and build strong financial health.

Ask yourself these questions:

- Can I handle this payment comfortably?
- What if my income changes or I face unexpected expenses?
- Do I have savings for emergencies or repairs?

A mortgage can build your future or weigh it down. The difference is understanding. Homeownership is not only about getting approved; it is about being ready.

When you know what to expect, you avoid costly mistakes, protect your finances, and enjoy becoming a homeowner.

The next chapters will walk you through how mortgages work, how credit affects your loan, and how to prepare for pre-approval. With the right knowledge, buying a home becomes not just possible but sustainable.

Chapter 2

Understanding How Mortgages Work

A mortgage is a loan used to buy a home. It is an agreement between a borrower and a lender in which the lender provides money and the borrower promises to repay it over time. Until the loan is fully paid, the lender has a legal interest in the property. This means the home serves as collateral.

Most mortgages in the United States are repaid over long terms, often fifteen or thirty years. Each monthly payment includes repayment of the amount borrowed and the cost of borrowing it. When managed wisely, a mortgage becomes a foundation for stability and future wealth. Without understanding, it can create financial strain. Knowing how this financial tool works helps buyers make choices that protect their future.

Key Elements of Mortgage Lending

A monthly mortgage payment has several parts. Understanding each one helps borrowers plan better and avoid surprises.

Principal
The principal is the amount borrowed to buy the home. Each monthly payment reduces this balance slowly over time.

Interest
Interest is the cost of borrowing money. It is how lenders earn income from the loan. The interest rate determines how much the loan costs over its lifetime.

Taxes
Property taxes are paid to local governments. Most lenders collect a portion of these taxes each month and place it in an escrow account to ensure timely payment.

Insurance
Homeowners insurance protects the property from loss or damage. Borrowers who make a small down payment may also pay mortgage insurance. This protects the lender but allows more people to qualify for homeownership.

These costs form the total mortgage payment. Knowing what each part covers help borrowers prepare for the full cost of owning a home.

How Lenders Decide

Before approving a mortgage, lenders review several factors that show whether a borrower can manage the loan responsibly. Each factor tells part of the borrower's financial story.

Credit Score
A good credit score shows that the borrower has handled past debts responsibly.

Higher scores often qualify for lower interest rates and more loan options.

Income
A stable and sufficient income reassures lenders that payments can be made without hardship. Pay stubs, tax returns, and other documents help verify income strength.

Debt to Income Ratio
This ratio compares monthly debt payments to monthly income. A lower ratio means the borrower has room in their budget for new obligations, which indicates stronger financial stability.

Employment History
A Consistent work history shows long term reliability. Job changes do not automatically disqualify a buyer if income remains steady and verifiable.

These factors help lenders make fair decisions. They also protect borrowers from taking on loans that might exceed their comfort or capacity.

Why Lenders Review Financial Information

Mortgage approval depends on the complete financial picture, not one detail alone. Lenders examine income, employment, credit, debts, savings, and the property itself. These combined details help determine if the borrower can manage payments comfortably.

The lender's goal is not to reject applicants but to match them with a loan they can sustain. Some people earn high incomes but carry large debts, while others have steady jobs but limited credit history. Each application is unique. Clear communication and early preparation prevent delays and build trust during the review process.

The Importance of Preparation

Many buyers start searching for homes before understanding what they can afford. This often leads to frustration or unexpected obstacles. Preparing financially before applying makes the experience smoother and more predictable.

Smart preparation steps include:

- Reviewing credit reports and correcting errors
- Keeping a steady record of on time payments
- Avoiding new debt before applying
- Saving for the down payment, closing costs, and reserves

- Organizing documents early
- Asking questions whenever something is unclear

Prepared buyers approach the process with confidence. Strong applications move more easily through review and approval, benefiting both borrower and lender.

A mortgage is more than a loan request. It is a long-term commitment built on planning, clear expectations, and honest communication. When borrowers understand how mortgages work, they take control of their financial journey and move toward lasting homeownership.

Chapter 3

How Mortgage Payments Are Calculated

Mortgage payments are shaped by several factors. The loan amount, interest rate, loan term, property taxes, and insurance all combine to determine the monthly cost. Seeing how these parts fit together helps borrowers plan and set realistic budgets.

For example, if someone borrows $300,000 for thirty years at a fixed interest rate, their monthly payment starts with two main pieces: principal and interest. As the loan balance drops, the principal portion gradually increases while the interest portion decreases. Property taxes and homeowners' insurance are then added to this base payment. These are usually collected monthly and held in an escrow account so they are paid when due.

Even if two borrowers take out the same loan amount, their payments may differ. Property taxes vary by location, and insurance costs change depending on the type of home, its value, and local risk factors. A house in one county may have higher taxes than a similar house elsewhere. Insurance can also be higher in areas with greater weather or replacement-cost risks.

A mortgage payment reflects more than the loan itself. It represents the full cost of owning and maintaining the property. Understanding this early prevents surprises and helps buyers plan beyond the purchase price.

Example – Monthly Mortgage Payment Breakdown

Loan amount: $300,000
Interest rate: 6.00 percent
Loan term: 30 years
Property taxes: $4,200 per year
Homeowners insurance: $1,200 per year
Mortgage type: Conventional loan

Step 1: Principal and Interest
A thirty-year fixed loan of $300,000 at 6 percent has a principal-and-interest payment of about $1,799 per month. This amount stays the same throughout the loan term. Over time, more of that payment goes toward principal and less toward interest.

Step 2: Property Taxes
Annual property taxes = $4,200
Monthly escrow amount = $350

Step 3: Homeowners Insurance
Annual premium = $1,200
Monthly portion = $100

Component	Monthly Amount
Principal and Interest	$1,799
Property Taxes	$350
Homeowners Insurance	$100
Total Monthly Payment	$2,249

Although the loan itself results in a payment of about $1,799, the full monthly obligation including taxes and insurance is roughly $2,249.

This shows why borrowers should always consider the complete payment, not just the loan amount.

Understanding Mortgage Amortization

Amortization is the schedule that shows how a mortgage is repaid over time.

In a thirty-year mortgage, the first few years focus mostly on interest, and the loan balance decreases slowly. Midway through the term, the principal portion becomes larger than the interest portion. In the final years, most of each payment reduces the remaining balance.

When borrowers understand amortization, they make better long-term choices.

They see why early progress feels slow and how consistent payments eventually build equity. Even small extra principal payments can shorten the loan and save thousands in interest.

Thirty-Year Amortization Overview ($300,000 loan at 6%)

Year	Approx. Loan Balance	Principal Paid That Year	Interest Paid That Year	Notes
1	$296,341	$3,659	$17,924	Mostly interest
5	$279,038	≈ $5,100	≈ $16,480	Principal increasing slowly
10	$251,213	≈ $8,200	≈ $14,980	Noticeable balance reduction
15	$212,820	≈ $11,900	≈ $13,180	Principal now greater than interest
20	$161,468	≈ $16,000	≈ $11,200	Strong equity growth
25	$94,000	≈ $21,000	≈ $8,600	Loan nearing completion

| 30 | $0 | Remaining balance cleared | Final interest portion | Loan fully paid |

Figures are approximate and shown for clarity.

A mortgage payment may stay the same each month, but how that payment is applied changes steadily. Early payments go mostly to interest, while later payments focus on principal. This gradual shift protects affordability and builds ownership over time.

What This Means for Homebuyers

- Early payments mostly cover interest
- Equity grows slowly at first, then faster later
- Staying in the home long term increases financial benefit
- Extra principal payments shorten the loan and reduce interest

Helpful Tip:

Making one extra principal payment per year, or simply rounding your monthly payment up can shorten a thirty-year loan by several years and save a significant amount in interest.

A mortgage does not reduce evenly. It follows a planned schedule that slowly moves in the borrower's favor. Understanding this structure keeps buyers confident and focused, especially during the early years when progress may seem slow.

Chapter 4

The Credit Connection

When you apply for a mortgage, the lender is not only deciding whether to approve your loan. They are also deciding how much risk they are taking by lending to you. That risk determines the interest rate you will pay.

Your credit score is one of the most powerful tools lenders use to measure that risk. A higher score shows a strong history of managing debt responsibly. A lower score signals possible trouble, such as missed payments or heavy debt. The difference between these two can mean thousands of dollars in savings or extra costs over the life of your mortgage.

Even small changes in your credit score can make a noticeable difference in your rate and monthly payment. That is why understanding creditworthiness is one of the most important parts of preparing for homeownership.

What Lenders Mean by Creditworthiness

Creditworthiness simply means how likely you are to repay borrowed money on time. Your credit report and credit score give lenders a snapshot of your borrowing habits, payment history, and overall financial behavior.

When reviewing your application, lenders also look at:
- Your payment history and any past late payments
- How much credit you currently use compared to your limits
- The types of credit accounts you have
- How long you have been using credit
- Any recent credit inquiries or new accounts

Lenders may also check for serious negative marks, such as bankruptcies, foreclosures, or collection accounts. These items do not automatically mean you will be denied, but they can affect your loan terms or increase your rate. In short, a high score shows consistency and reliability. A low score tells a lender that lending to you may carry more risk.

Typical Credit Score Ranges

While lenders use several scoring models, most rely on a version of the FICO® score.

Here's how the general ranges are viewed:

Credit Range	Score Range	Typical View by Lenders
Exceptional	800 – 850	Lowest risk, best rates
Very Good	740 – 799	Strong borrower, competitive rates
Good	670 – 739	Average borrower, reasonable terms
Fair	580 – 669	Some challenges, higher rates likely

| Poor | 300 – 579 | Significant credit risk, limited options |

Buyers with scores in the "good" to "excellent" range usually qualify for the most favorable terms. Those with lower scores often face higher rates to offset the lender's risk.

Although requirements vary by loan type and lender, many follow these general guidelines:

- 620 or higher for most conventional loans
- 580 and above for many FHA loans
- 620 to 640 for most USDA loans
- VA loans do not set a minimum score by rule, but most lenders prefer at least 620

Recent industry updates now allow lenders to consider positive data such as rental, utility, and mobile phone payment history. This gives responsible borrowers more ways to show financial reliability.

Why Credit Scores Affect Interest Rates

Lenders use a method called risk-based pricing. This means that interest rates are adjusted based on the likelihood of repayment.

If a borrower has a high credit score, it shows a strong record of paying bills on time and managing accounts responsibly. Since this borrower is considered less risky, the lender can offer a lower rate.

If another borrower has a lower credit score, the lender views them as a higher risk.
They may have late payments, high debts, or limited credit history. To protect themselves, the lender charges a higher rate.

This difference in risk is what separates a 6.0% mortgage from a 7.5% one, even on the same loan amount. Over time, that small difference can amount to tens of thousands of dollars.

How a Low Credit Score Increases Costs

A low credit score can increase borrowing costs in several ways:
- Higher interest rate — even a 1% increase can raise payments by hundreds of dollars
- Higher insurance premiums — some insurers use credit history when setting rates
- Larger required down payment — to offset higher risk
- Limited loan program choices

It's important to remember that a low score is not permanent. With time and consistent effort, anyone can rebuild their credit profile.

How a High Credit Score Saves Money

A high credit score signals trust and stability. Lenders are confident that you will repay your loan, so they reward you with lower rates and better terms.

With excellent credit, you can often:
- Qualify for lower interest rates
- Reduce your total loan costs
- Access more loan programs
- Pay less for insurance and fees

Borrowers with strong credit histories save thousands over the life of their loan. The effort to build good credit always pays off.

Common Credit Mistakes That Cost Borrowers Thousands

Many borrowers unintentionally slow their progress by making these mistakes:
1. Maxing out credit cards before applying
2. Closing older accounts, which shortens credit history
3. Allowing small bills to go to collections
4. Applying for multiple credit cards or loans in a short time
5. Assuming online credit scores are the same as lender-pulled scores

Real-World Credit Challenges

Credit Freezes, Disputes, and Identity Protection

As data breaches become more common, many people use credit freezes or fraud alerts for protection. While this is smart, it can delay a mortgage application if not managed early. If your credit is frozen, your lender cannot access your report. This can delay pre-approval or underwriting until the freeze is lifted.

Before applying:

- Lift or temporarily thaw credit freezes with all three bureaus
- Resolve any ongoing disputes on your credit report
- Monitor reports for errors and fraudulent accounts

These steps help avoid delays and protect your credit during the mortgage process.

Co-Signing Loans for Others

Co-signing a loan affects your credit as if it were your own. If the primary borrower misses payments, your score will also drop. It can inflate your debt-to-income ratio and lower your qualification amount.

Helpful Tip: Avoid co-signing new loans if you plan to buy a home soon. If you already have, keep proof of on-time payments and inform your loan officer. Clear records help during underwriting.

Student Loan Debt and Mortgage Qualification

Many potential homebuyers carry student loan balances that affect their ability to qualify. Lenders count student loan payments as part of monthly debt, even if they are deferred or income-based.

This often surprises borrowers who assume paused or reduced payments don't count.

Even small payments can affect your qualification amount.

What you can do:

- Ask your loan officer how your servicer reports payment.
- Provide documentation showing your actual monthly payment
- If you use an income-based repayment plan, confirm that it qualifies for underwriting
- Avoid deferring or consolidating loans during the process without lender guidance

Proper planning helps borrowers with student debt qualify responsibly.

How to Improve Your Credit Score Before Applying

Even if your score isn't perfect, you can strengthen it before applying for a mortgage. Improvement takes time but brings lasting benefits.

1. Check your credit report regularly.
   Get free copies from annualcreditreport.com or the credit bureaus. Review for accuracy and dispute errors.

2. Pay all bills on time.
   Payment history has the biggest impact on your score. Use reminders or automatic payments.

3. Keep balances low.
   Try to use less than thirty percent of available credit. Borrowers with excellent credit often stay below ten percent.

4. Avoid new debt before applying.
   Each new inquiry or account can temporarily lower your score.

5. Keep older accounts open.
   The length of your credit history matters. Closing old accounts can reduce your average credit age.

6. Build positive credit activity.
   Services like rent or utility reporting can help show consistent payment habits.

7. Seek professional guidance if needed.
   A certified credit counselor or loan officer can help you create a clear plan for improvement.

Your credit score shows how you have managed money and responsibility over time.

This history directly affects what you will pay for your home. Buyers who learn about and improve their credit have an advantage; they qualify for better rates, save money each month, and build equity faster.

Good credit is not only about getting approved. It means having options, confidence, and long-term savings.

Example: How Credit Affects Mortgage Costs

Loan Amount: $300,000
Loan Term: 30 years (360 months)

Credit Score Range	Approx. Rate	Monthly Payment (P&I)	Total Interest Over 30 Years	Total Cost (Principal + Interest)
Excellent (760–850)	6.00%	$1,799	$347,515	$647,515
Good (700–759)	6.50%	$1,896	$382,560	$682,560
Fair (640–699)	7.25%	$2,047	$437,150	$737,150
Poor (580–639)	8.50%	$2,314	$532,080	$832,080

What the Chart Shows

A small change in your credit score can have a major financial effect. The borrower with excellent credit pays about $1,799 a month, while one with poor credit pays $2,314. That is a difference of more than $184,000 over the life of the loan.

Every point on your credit score matters. Improving it before applying can mean lower payments, less stress, and faster financial freedom. Having good credit not only helps you buy a home; it gives you peace of mind.

Quick Credit Readiness Checklist

Before applying for a mortgage, review your financial readiness.

Check each box that applies to you:

- ☐ I have reviewed and understand my current credit score.
- ☐ I have made no late payments in the past twelve months.
- ☐ My credit card balances are below thirty percent of the limit.
- ☐ I have avoided taking on new debt recently.
- ☐ I have a savings plan for my down payment and reserves.
- ☐ I have checked my credit report for errors.
- ☐ My work history and income are stable.
- ☐ I have a plan to avoid major financial changes before closing.

Chapter 5

Preparing for Pre-Approval

One of the most important steps in getting a mortgage is getting pre-approved. This is where your dream starts to come true and where lenders look closely at your finances for the first time.

A lot of people think that pre-approval is just a quick formality, but it's not. The lender uses pre-approval to check that you can afford a mortgage. It also helps you shop for homes with confidence within your budget by giving you a clear picture of how much you can afford.

What It Means to Be Pre-Approved

When you are pre-approved, the lender looks at your income, assets, debts, and credit to figure out how much you can borrow and what the terms will be.
A pre-approval letter gives you an edge over other buyers, especially in busy markets. When sellers see that a lender has already looked at your finances, they are more likely to take your offer seriously.

Documents and Details You Will Need to Get Started

To obtain pre-approval, borrowers typically provide:
• Recent pay stubs
• W-2 forms or tax returns
• Bank statements
• Identification documents
• Information on outstanding loans and monthly debts
• Employment details
• Explanation of any unusual financial activity

If you are self-employed, you might be required to submit financial records, such as profit-and-loss statements and business tax returns. This helps the lender verify steady income and money management. Documents that are well organized make the process quicker.

How to Calculate How Much Home You Can Afford

To determine how much a borrower can qualify for, lenders consider factors such as income, credit, and current obligations. But affordability is more than just qualifications. Personal comfort matters too. A lender might authorize a larger monthly payment than a borrower feels comfortable making.

Many professionals follow the guideline that housing expenses should not exceed a fair portion of gross income each month. Future costs like maintenance, emergency savings, and personal goals should also be taken into account. Long-term comfort, not just loan approval, ensures stability.

Realistic Expectations Versus Emotional Excitement

It can be very emotional to buy a house. Once the search starts, the excitement builds quickly. It's normal to be excited, but staying grounded helps avoid money problems. Some buyers want the biggest loan possible without thinking about long-term stability. Others compare themselves to friends, family, or online stories without realizing their situations differ.

Realistic expectations lead to smart choices. Buying a home that is well planned feels good and is easy to handle. Too much enthusiasm can make it feel like a burden. Being patient and clear is more important than being quick.

Real-World Pre-Approval Related Challenges

Income Inconsistencies and Fluctuations:
One of the most common problems during pre-approval is income that isn't steady.

Many buyers, especially those who work for themselves, on commission, or receive bonuses, have income that changes from month to month.

Lenders like income that is steady and predictable because it shows stability. If your income changes, the lender will review your past two years and average it to find stability. If income went down, the lender might use the lower figure.

Tips to Handle This Challenge:

- Keep detailed records of income, invoices, and deposits.
- Save extra during strong months to balance slower ones.
- Avoid large unexplained deposits or transfers.
- Be transparent with your loan officer about side or gig income.

Self-Employed Borrowers and Documentation:
Getting pre-approved can seem more difficult if you run your own company or are self-employed, but it is completely doable with the right planning.
Usually, self-employed borrowers provide two years of full tax returns, including all schedules. Lenders look at net income after deductions. When tax planning lowers taxable income, it can also lower borrowing capacity.

How to Strengthen Your Position:

- Maintain separate business and personal bank accounts.
- Keep business expenses well documented.
- Avoid writing off excessive expenses before applying.
- Prepare year-to-date profit-and-loss statements if requested.
- Be ready to explain any business losses or irregularities.

Planning ahead helps self-employed buyers succeed. Lenders will view your income as reliable if records are clear and consistent.

Documentation Red Flags:
Even small mistakes on your paperwork can cause delays. Missing pages, unexplained deposits, or differences between documents may require re-verification.

If you make a large deposit without showing its source, you may be asked more questions. Lenders must ensure that funds used for down payment or closing are legal and traceable.

To Avoid Red Flags:

- Do not move large sums between accounts before approval.
- Keep a paper trail for all transfers or gifts.
- Avoid changing jobs during the process.
- Respond quickly to lender requests.

Think of your documentation as your financial story. The clearer the story, the faster the approval.

Emotional Pressure During Pre-Approval

It can be stressful to wait for news, worry about credit checks, and gather paperwork. Some borrowers feel anxious before approval because they fear something will go wrong.
It's normal to feel this way. The process is private, and money matters are sensitive.

How to Manage the Emotional Side:

- Work with a loan officer who communicates clearly.
- Avoid comparing your situation to others.
- Remember that pre-approval is not judgment, it is preparation.
- Stay patient and organized.

Pre-approval is the step that turns uncertainty into opportunity, but it can also test your patience. The more you know, the less stress you feel.

Life Scenario – When the Paperwork Almost Ruined the Deal

Tina was a freelance designer who had worked for many clients. She proudly sent her income reports and bank statements when she applied for pre-approval, her loan officer discovered that most payments went into a joint account she shared with her sister; so, they could not verify which deposits were hers, delaying approval by two weeks.

She resubmitted invoices and separated business deposits, and the loan was approved.
Tina learned that being organized is just as important as earning money. Even strong income can appear weak if documentation is unclear.

To Make Things Go Smoothly:

- Be honest with your lender from the start.
- Keep all financial papers up to date and ready.
- Avoid major financial changes until after closing.
- Expect that some delays and requests are normal.

Every successful homeowner has been in your shoes, wondering if everything would go well. Being ready, patient, and communicative makes all the difference.

Pre-Approval Checklist

Before starting, make sure you can check off the following:

☑ Steady income and verifiable employment
☑ Clear and accurate financial documents
☑ No major credit changes or new loans
☑ Saved funds for down payment and closing costs
☑ Emotional readiness to handle the process

Pre-approval is not the finish line; it is the green light that says, "You are ready to begin your homebuying journey."

Loan Officer's Advice – How to Spot Red Flags Early

Experienced loan officers recognize signs that may delay approval. Common red flags include:

- Sudden job changes without a clear career path
- Large unexplained deposits shortly before application
- High revolving debt balances
- Multiple recent credit inquiries
- Inconsistent income history
- Limited reserve funds or no emergency savings

Borrowers can fix problems early if they identify them quickly. Clear communication and planning make the file stronger and protect the borrower's interests.

Chapter 6

How To Choose the Right Mortgage

There are several mortgage programs available in the United States. Each one serves a different type of borrower and situation. Understanding the differences helps buyers choose wisely and allows loan officers to guide clients based on their financial goals and long-term plans.

Fixed Rate Mortgage

A fixed rate loan keeps the same interest rate for the entire term of the loan. Monthly payments remain steady and predictable. This option works well for borrowers who plan to stay in their home long term and want consistent payments without future surprises.

Adjustable-Rate Mortgage

An adjustable-rate mortgage begins with a set interest rate for a specific number of years. After that period, the rate can change at scheduled intervals. Adjustable loans can offer lower initial rates, but future payments may rise depending on market conditions. They fit buyers who expect to move or refinance before the adjustment period begins and who can manage changes in payment amounts if needed.

FHA Loan

FHA loans are supported by the Federal Housing Administration. They allow buyers to qualify with more flexible credit and lower down payment requirements, usually as low as 3.5 percent. Mortgage insurance is required to protect the lender. FHA loans are popular among first-time homebuyers and those building their financial history.

VA Loan

VA loans are offered to eligible service members, veterans, and certain surviving spouses. These loans often require no down payment and have no monthly mortgage insurance. They usually include lower rates and flexible credit standards. The VA funding fee may apply but can often be rolled into the loan. VA loans are one of the strongest benefits available to those who have served the country.

USDA Loan

USDA loans are designed for eligible rural and suburban areas. They also offer no down payment options for qualified borrowers. Income and property location guidelines apply. Many buyers are surprised to learn that some suburban neighborhoods qualify as USDA eligible. These loans require an upfront and annual guarantee fee similar to mortgage insurance.

Conventional Loan

Conventional loans are not backed by the government. They typically require stronger credit and financial stability but offer competitive terms and flexible options. Down payments can be as low as 3 percent for qualified first-time buyers. Borrowers who put down at least 20 percent can avoid mortgage insurance entirely. Conventional loans are available in both conforming and jumbo versions, depending on the loan amount.

Jumbo Loans

Jumbo loans are used when the loan amount exceeds the limits set by Fannie Mae and Freddie Mac, known as *conforming loan limits*. These loans are often used to finance luxury or high-cost properties. Because they involve larger balances, jumbo loans may require higher credit scores, bigger down payments, and strong documentation of income and assets.

Renovation and Specialty Loans

Some buyers purchase homes that need updates or repairs. Programs like the FHA 203(k) or Fannie Mae Home Style loans allow financing for both the purchase price and renovation costs in a single mortgage. These programs help turn fixer-uppers into dream homes without requiring a separate construction loan.

How to Match the Right Loan to Your Long-Term Goals

A mortgage should fit your lifestyle, finances, and future plans. A fixed-rate loan may suit someone who plans to stay in the same home for many years. An adjustable-rate loan may appeal to a borrower expecting to relocate or refinance within a shorter time frame.

The right loan depends on:
- How long you plan to own the home
- Comfort with potential payment changes
- Down payment ability
- Credit strength
- Plans for refinancing or upgrading later

Financial goals should guide loan selection, not short-term advertisements or limited-time offers.

Down Payment and Mortgage Insurance at a Glance

Loan Type	Minimum Down Payment	Mortgage Insurance Required?	Notes
Conventional	3% (first-time buyers)	Yes, if under 20% down	Can be removed when equity reaches 20%
FHA	3.5%	Yes, for life of loan (unless refinanced)	Easier credit standards

VA	0%	No	Funding fee may apply
USDA	0%	Yes, annual and upfront fees	Limited to eligible areas
Jumbo	10–20% typical	Often no	Stricter credit and asset standards

Understanding these differences helps borrowers plan realistic savings goals and choose what fits their situation best.

The Hidden Traps in Low Interest or No Money Down Offers

Some advertisements highlight low starting rates or no down payment options. While appealing, they may include features that raise long-term costs. Adjustable rates may rise sooner than expected, and low-down payment loans may include lifetime mortgage insurance or higher fees. Always review the full loan estimate before deciding.

Interest Rate vs. APR

The interest rate is the cost of borrowing money. The APR (Annual Percentage Rate) includes the interest rate plus fees and other costs over the loan term. Comparing APRs between lenders helps you see which offer is truly less expensive overall.

Rate Locks and Timing

Interest rates can change daily. A rate lock protects you from market changes for a set period; usually 30 to 60 days while your loan closes. Locking in a rate can prevent surprises, especially in rising rate markets. Ask your lender how long your rate lock lasts and if extensions cost extra.

First-Time Homebuyer and Assistance Programs

Many state and local housing agencies offer grants, forgivable loans, or down payment assistance for eligible first-time buyers. These programs often combine with FHA, VA, or Conventional loans to reduce upfront costs. Loan officers can help identify available programs based on location and income.

Refinancing Basics

Refinancing allows homeowners to replace an existing mortgage with a new one, often to lower the rate, shorten the term, or remove mortgage insurance. Most FHA, VA, and Conventional loans allow refinancing. Borrowers should compare total costs and consider how long they plan to stay in the home before refinancing.

How Loan Officers Can Guide Buyers to Safe, Smart Choices

A loan officer's role is to provide clear explanations and compare loan programs side by side. Buyers rely on professionals to explain interest structures, costs, and timelines. A responsible loan officer asks about future plans, job stability, and financial goals. Good communication protects clients from confusion and builds trust through transparency.

Comparison Chart – Short-Term vs. Long-Term Loan Benefits

Loan Type Focus	Advantages	Considerations
Shorter term loan (15 years)	Faster payoff, lower total interest, builds equity quickly	Higher monthly payment, less cash flexibility
Longer term loan (30 years)	Lower monthly payment, more room in budget	Higher total interest cost over time

The best mortgage is not always the one with the lowest rate; it's the one that matches your financial comfort, long-term plans, and ability to manage payments confidently.

Understanding each loan type and asking the right questions gives buyers control over their decisions and peace of mind.

Chapter 7

Shopping for a Lender, Not Just a Loan

Borrowers today have more choices than ever when deciding where to get a mortgage. Each type of lender operates differently, offers unique benefits, and serves different kinds of buyers. Understanding how these lenders work helps borrowers make smart, confident decisions that match their financial goals and comfort level.

Banks

Banks are the traditional choice for many homebuyers. They offer mortgage loans along with checking, savings, and other financial products. Borrowers who already have accounts with a bank may benefit from loyalty rate programs or relationship discounts.

Banks are known for stability and clear procedures, but their mortgage programs can be more limited compared to independent lenders. Because they follow strict internal guidelines, approval may take longer and require more documentation. Still, for borrowers who value in-person service and established reputations, banks can be a dependable option.

Mortgage Brokers

Mortgage brokers act as matchmakers between borrowers and lenders. Instead of lending money directly, brokers shop around with multiple lenders to find loan programs that fit a client's financial profile. This access to variety allows borrowers to compare interest rates, terms, and closing costs more efficiently.

A skilled broker simplifies the process by handling paperwork, comparing offers, and negotiating on the borrower's behalf. The quality of service, however, depends on the broker's experience and network. Borrowers should always ask how brokers are compensated and confirm that the broker's recommendations are based on the borrower's best interest, not higher commissions.

Credit Unions

Credit unions are nonprofit, member-based institutions that often provide competitive interest rates and low fees. Because they focus on community and member relationships, their service tends to be more personal.

Many credit unions also offer programs tailored to first-time buyers or members with moderate incomes. Membership is required, but joining is usually simple. For borrowers who prefer a smaller, relationship-driven experience, credit unions are often a great choice.

Online Mortgage Platforms

Technology has changed how people apply for mortgages. Online lenders and digital platforms allow borrowers to complete applications, upload documents, and track progress entirely online.

This convenience appeals to many modern buyers who want faster responses and 24/7 access. However, while rates can be competitive, the experience varies. Some borrowers prefer personal guidance, and online communication may feel less supportive when questions arise. The best approach is to choose a platform that combines digital efficiency with responsive customer service.

Choosing What Works Best for You

The best lender is the one that fits your comfort level, finances, and long-term goals. A first-time buyer may appreciate the support of a broker or credit union, while an experienced homeowner might prefer the convenience of an online platform. Comparing more than one option helps borrowers see the full range of rates, fees, and service styles available.

Understanding Rates, Fees, and the Fine Print

The interest rate is a major factor in your mortgage, but it is not the whole story. Every loan comes with additional costs that affect the total amount you'll pay. Borrowers should review all parts of the Loan Estimate carefully, including:

- Origination or application fees
- Discount points (optional prepaid interest to lower your rate)
- Appraisal and underwriting fees
- Title and closing costs
- Mortgage insurance (if required)
- Prepaid taxes and homeowners' insurance

Two loans with the same rate can have very different total costs. Comparing the **Annual Percentage Rate (APR)** rather than just the interest rate gives a more accurate picture of what the loan will truly cost over time. The APR includes both the rate and lender fees, which makes it easier to compare offers from different institutions.

A careful review of these details helps borrowers avoid unpleasant surprises at closing and ensures that the loan fits within their financial comfort zone.

Negotiating for Better Terms

Many borrowers assume that loan terms are fixed, but that is not always the case. Certain costs and features can be negotiated. It never hurts to ask your lender or broker about:

- Lower origination or processing fees
- Credits toward closing costs
- Rate lock extensions or float-down options
- Discounts for automatic payments or strong credit profiles

Market competition often gives lenders some flexibility. Borrowers who are polite but proactive can sometimes save thousands simply by asking questions and showing that they are comparing multiple offers.

Watch Out for Misleading Offers

Not every attractive advertisement tells the full story. Some lenders promote extremely low rates that are available only to borrowers with perfect credit, high income, or by paying expensive discount points upfront. Others claim "no closing costs," but roll those expenses into a higher loan balance or higher interest rate.

One borrower once chose a lender based on an online ad for an unusually low rate. Only later did they learn that the advertised offer required paying thousands in extra fees. By then, they had already invested time and emotional energy in the process.

Taking a moment to read the fine print and ask direct questions early on can prevent this kind of situation.

What Experienced Loan Officers Wish Borrowers Knew

Loan officers want borrowers to succeed. The most successful homebuyers are those who come prepared, ask questions, and understand the basics of how mortgages work. Here are a few points every professional wish new buyers would remember:

- Interest rates change daily and depend on market conditions.
- Not every loan program fits every borrower.
- Pre-approval is a strong start but not a final commitment.
- Your loan should fit your long-term comfort, not just short-term affordability.
- Transparency and communication with your loan officer make the process faster and smoother.

Informed borrowers experience fewer surprises, close faster, and make choices that protect their financial health.

Choosing the right lender is about more than finding the lowest rate. It's about building a relationship with a trusted professional who explains clearly, answers questions honestly, and helps you make decisions that strengthen your financial foundation.

When you understand your options and read the fine print carefully, you take control of your mortgage journey, and that's where real confidence begins.

Chapter 8

The Loan Process Step by Step

The mortgage process has many moving parts, and each one plays a crucial role. While it may sometimes feel detailed or slow, every step exists to protect the borrower and ensure a successful home purchase. A strong start, steady communication, and clear expectations allow both buyers and loan officers to move forward with confidence.

A mortgage is more than a stack of paperwork. It is a structured plan that balances financial preparation, property evaluation, and responsible lending. When everyone involved understands their role and communicates openly, the experience becomes smoother and less stressful.

Below is a complete walkthrough of what happens between your first conversation with a lender and the day you receive the keys.

The Stages of the Mortgage Process

Although the process looks straightforward, each stage contains important checks and approvals that work together to protect everyone involved.

The main steps are:
1. Initial consultation with a loan professional
2. Verified pre-approval
3. Home search and accepted offer
4. Full loan application
5. Processing and document review
6. Appraisal and property verification
7. Underwriting
8. Final approval, also known as "clear to close"
9. Loan closing and transfer of ownership

Borrowers who understand these steps in advance move through them more comfortably and are better prepared to respond quickly to lender requests.

Step 1: Initial Consultation

The process begins with a conversation between the borrower and a loan professional. The loan officer reviews income, assets, and goals, then outlines what loan programs may be available. This step helps the borrower understand what to expect and prepares them for documentation and budgeting. Even if a buyer is not ready to purchase immediately, this early discussion sets a strong foundation and helps identify any issues that should be addressed before moving forward.

Step 2: Pre-Approval

Once financial details are verified, the borrower receives a pre-approval letter.

This document confirms the lender has reviewed income, assets, and credit history and is prepared to move forward when the right property is found. Pre-approval helps buyers focus on homes within their true price range and gives sellers confidence that the offer is genuine.

Step 3: Finding a Home and Getting an Accepted Offer

After pre-approval, the buyer works with a real estate agent to find a suitable home. When an offer is accepted, the mortgage file becomes tied to that specific property. The lender then begins reviewing the home's value, title history, and condition to ensure it qualifies for financing.

This step combines both financial and property evaluation. While exciting, it also requires patience as the lender verifies that the property is sound and meets loan requirements.

Step 4: Completing the Full Loan Application

Once the offer is accepted, the buyer completes the full mortgage application. At this point, the lender collects all required documents—income verification, asset statements, identification, and property information.

The file is then assigned to a loan processor, who checks that everything is accurate and complete. The processor ensures all details meet lending standards and prepares the file for underwriting. Quick, organized responses from borrowers make this stage faster and less stressful.

Step 5: Processing and Documentation

During processing, the lender may request updated bank statements, employment verification, or explanations for certain transactions. These requests are routine and help confirm that the borrower's financial situation has not changed.

Timely communication is key. Delays in providing documents can extend the timeline or create unnecessary pressure. A responsive borrower keeps the process on track and builds trust with the lender.

Step 6: Appraisal and Property Review

An appraisal is ordered to confirm that the home's value supports the loan amount. It protects both the buyer and the lender by ensuring the property is worth the agreed purchase price.

The appraiser evaluates comparable recent sales, property condition, and location. In some loan programs, the lender may also review basic safety and habitability standards. If repairs or adjustments are needed, the loan officer and real estate agent help the buyer navigate solutions quickly.

Appraisals are not personal judgments; they are part of responsible lending and protect the buyer from overpaying.

Step 7: Underwriting Review

Underwriting is the most technical stage of the process. The underwriter reviews the complete file to confirm it meets all lending, legal, and regulatory requirements.

They verify that income is stable, assets are legitimate, credit behavior is consistent, and the property meets standards. If something is missing or unclear, the underwriter may issue a "conditional approval," requesting additional clarification or documents.

This step can feel intense, but it is routine. Underwriting exists to ensure that both the borrower and the lender are protected.

Step 8: Clear to Close

Once the underwriter confirms that every condition is met, the loan is officially "clear to close." This means the final documentation is approved, and closing can be scheduled.

At this point, the borrower receives the Closing Disclosure, which outlines the final interest rate, payment details, and closing costs. Borrowers should review this document carefully, ask questions, and confirm that everything matches earlier loan estimates.

Reaching "clear to close" is a major milestone; it reflects financial readiness, accuracy, and strong teamwork.

Step 9: Closing and Receiving the Keys

Closing day is when all parties sign the final documents and funds are released. The title company or closing attorney ensures that legal ownership is transferred correctly. Once funds are disbursed, the buyer receives the keys and officially becomes a homeowner.

It's the last step in the lending journey and the first step into homeownership. Preparation, honesty, and timely communication make this day smooth and rewarding.

Maintaining Stability During the Process

Between application and closing, financial stability is essential. Borrowers should avoid making big financial changes until after closing. This includes changing jobs, taking on new debt, moving large sums of money, or missing any payments. Even positive actions like paying off a loan early should be discussed with the lender before proceeding.

Lenders verify every major financial event, so consistency and transparency are key to keeping the process on track.

The Role of Communication and Transparency

A mortgage is built on trust and accurate information. Loan officers rely on honest, consistent communication to move the loan safely through each stage. When borrowers share updates, ask questions, and stay responsive, any issue can be solved quickly.

Silence, guessing, or withholding information only creates confusion or delays. Borrowers should never hesitate to reach out for clarification. Mortgage professionals are there to guide every step and ensure that the experience is educational, transparent, and empowering.

The mortgage process is not just about approval; it is about understanding, preparation, and teamwork. Every stage has a purpose, and when approached with patience and communication, it leads to the best possible outcome.

A smooth mortgage process begins with honesty, continues with consistency, and ends with the moment you receive the keys to your new home.

Chapter 9

Common Mortgage Mistakes and How to Avoid Them

The mortgage process rewards preparation, patience, and understanding. Most challenges buyers face do not come from the market or even the lender. They often come from decisions made too quickly or without the right information. Avoiding these common mistakes protects your finances and creates a smoother path to homeownership.

Loan officers have seen the same patterns over time. Buyers who take the time to learn and plan make better decisions, move through the process more confidently, and experience fewer surprises. The following sections highlight frequent mistakes and explain how to prevent them.

Applying for Loans Without Pre-Approval

Many eager buyers begin touring homes before securing pre-approval. While the excitement of searching is understandable, skipping this step can lead to frustration.

Pre-approval gives you a clear price range, confirms that financing is in place, and strengthens your negotiation power with sellers. Without it, buyers risk focusing on homes outside their affordable range or losing to others who are already pre-approved.

Pre-approval is not just a formality; it is your financial starting point. It ensures that when you find the right home, you can act with confidence and speed.

Taking Verbal Promises as Binding Agreements

Verbal promises do not hold weight in mortgage lending. Interest rates, credits, and closing timelines must always be documented in writing. A conversation or casual assurance is not the same as a binding agreement.

Borrowers should always request written confirmation for key items such as:

- Rate quotes and fee structures
- Approval conditions or contingencies
- Estimated closing schedules
- Any special credits or negotiated terms

Having everything documented ensures clarity and prevents confusion later. Clear records protect both the borrower and the lender, making sure expectations match reality.

Falling for "Too Good to Be True" Offers

Some advertisements or online lenders promote extremely low interest rates to capture attention.

However, these offers often come with hidden conditions, high fees, or are available only to borrowers with exceptional credit and large down payments.

Responsible borrowers should review:

- The combination of rate, points, and lender fees
- Details in the Loan Estimate
- The full term of the loan, including adjustable features or prepayment penalties
- The licensing and reputation of the lender

If an offer seems unusually low compared to others, ask what specific requirements are attached. The lowest rate is not always the best loan. What matters is the total cost and how it fits your long-term financial comfort.

Borrowing Beyond Financial Comfort

A lender can calculate how much you *qualify* for, but only you know how much you can *comfortably manage*. Borrowers sometimes focus on the maximum approved amount instead of what fits their real lifestyle and savings goals.

It's important to think beyond the monthly payment and consider:

- Emergency savings and future expenses
- Maintenance costs and property taxes

- Personal lifestyle priorities, such as travel, education, or childcare
- The long-term financial flexibility you want to maintain

The best mortgage supports your life rather than limits it. Borrow within a range that lets you build equity while keeping room for unexpected changes.

Changing Employment or Finances During the Process

Financial stability is one of the most important factors during the mortgage process. Lenders verify your income and assets at the beginning and again before closing. Sudden changes like switching jobs, taking on new debt, or making large purchases can delay or even cancel your approval.

Before making any major financial move, talk with your loan officer. Even positive changes, such as paying off a debt or receiving a bonus, can affect how your application is evaluated.

Communication ensures your actions support your loan approval, not complicate it.

Misunderstanding Mortgage Insurance and Down Payments

Many buyers assume that a large down payment is the only way to qualify for a mortgage, while others expect to buy with little or no money down. In truth, there are flexible options for both.

Low down payment programs often include mortgage insurance, which adds to the monthly cost but allows buyers to enter the market sooner. On the other hand, larger down payments can reduce or remove that insurance cost altogether.

The key is understanding how your choice affects both your short-term payment and long-term savings. A loan officer can help you compare scenarios side by side to find the most balanced option for your goals.

Not Comparing Lenders or Loan Options

A mortgage is one of the largest financial decisions you will make, and not all lenders are the same. Rates, fees, and service levels vary across institutions. Borrowers who compare at least two or three lenders often find meaningful savings or better support.

When comparing, look beyond interest rates. Consider the lender's communication style, transparency, and ability to explain complex terms clearly. The right lender is not just the cheapest one; it's the one who helps you feel informed and supported.

The Loan Officer's Role in Protecting Borrowers

A professional loan officer is more than a salesperson. They are a guide who helps borrowers avoid costly mistakes and make confident choices. A good loan officer will:

- Encourage pre-approval early in the process
- Explain all costs, not just the interest rate
- Review credit and finances thoroughly
- Ask about your long-term goals and comfort level
- Confirm understanding before final commitments

Their goal is not simply to close a loan but to ensure that each borrower enters homeownership responsibly and sustainably.

Key Reminders for Borrowers

Successful homebuyers share one common trait; they prepare. Keep these reminders in mind as you begin your journey:

- Plan before searching for a home
- Get everything in writing, including rates and fees
- Avoid major financial changes before closing
- Compare multiple lenders and programs
- Focus on long-term comfort, not short-term excitement

Being informed is the best protection you have. Every careful decision you make today helps secure a more stable and rewarding future as a homeowner.

Chapter 10

The Emotional Side of Homebuying

Buying a home is one of the most meaningful financial and personal decisions most people ever make. It is far more than a transaction. It represents belonging, stability, pride, and a sense of achievement. Because of this, the mortgage process carries emotion as well as logic. Excitement, hope, fear, and stress often surface at different points along the journey.

Recognizing these emotions helps buyers remain balanced and allows loan officers to guide with empathy and patience. When emotions are understood instead of ignored, decisions become stronger, and the homebuying experience becomes far more rewarding.

Why Homebuying Feels So Emotional

A home is not just a structure; it is a reflection of comfort, safety, and identity. Buyers imagine future memories inside its walls, and that connection creates deep emotional investment long before the purchase is complete.

Common emotional moments include:

- Excitement when beginning the search
- Anxiety about competition or rising prices
- Doubt during negotiations or document review
- Stress as deadlines approach
- Relief and pride at closing

These emotions are normal. They reflect how personal and significant the homebuying process truly is. Understanding them helps buyers remain calm, patient, and focused even during uncertainty.

How Emotions Affect Decision-Making

Emotions can strengthen or weaken decision-making depending on how they are managed. Awareness helps buyers avoid impulsive choices and maintain perspective.

Fear
Fear can lead to hesitation or overthinking. Some buyers delay taking action because they worry about making a mistake or not understanding every detail. Fear is natural but should not control the process. The best way to reduce it is to stay informed, ask questions, and rely on professional guidance.

Stress
Deadlines, paperwork, and communication with multiple parties can create tension. When stress

builds, buyers may rush through documents or overlook important details. Staying organized and keeping an open line of communication with your loan officer helps maintain clarity and calm.

Excitement
Excitement is often the first emotion in homebuying. It can be motivating, but it can also encourage impulsive decisions like falling in love with a home that stretches the budget or overlooking a long commute. Excitement should inspire action, not replace careful evaluation. The best decisions come when enthusiasm is balanced with patience.

Balanced emotions support smart choices. Buyers who acknowledge how they feel can pause, reflect, and make decisions that align with their long-term comfort.

The Loan Officer's Role: A Guide and Steady Voice

A great loan officer does more than process paperwork or quote interest rates. They serve as a guide who brings clarity when things feel uncertain. Their calm, professional voice helps keep the process grounded when emotions rise.

Loan officers can support clients by:

- Explaining each step clearly and avoiding unnecessary jargon

- Setting realistic timelines and expectations
- Encouraging patience when the process feels slow
- Offering reassurance during moments of uncertainty
- Helping clients stay focused on the long-term benefits of ownership

Good lending is not only about numbers; it's about relationships built on trust and open communication. Buyers value professionals who listen, explain, and stay steady when emotions fluctuate.

Helping Buyers Stay Grounded

Buying a home can be exciting, but it also requires emotional discipline. Here are practical ways for buyers to stay centered and confident:

- Review long-term goals before starting the home search
- Set a clear budget and avoid exceeding it
- Ask questions early to remove doubt or confusion
- Take short breaks during stressful moments
- Keep written priorities nearby to guide decisions
- Avoid comparing your progress or timeline with others

Every homebuying journey is unique. Comparing yourself to others can create pressure that doesn't reflect your financial reality. A well-prepared buyer who moves at their own pace will experience less stress and greater satisfaction in the end.

The Value of Patience and Perspective

A home purchase is a major commitment that deserves time and thought. Rushing to meet emotional expectations or market pressure can lead to regret. Patience allows you to evaluate your choices fully and move forward when you are truly ready.

Perspective is equally important. Every small delay or additional document request is part of a process designed to protect you. Buying a home wisely means focusing not just on closing quickly but on closing confidently.

The mortgage journey rewards those who combine patience with preparation. The goal is not just to own a home; it is to own one with peace of mind, knowing the decision was thoughtful, informed, and right for your life.

The emotional side of buying a home is powerful, but it doesn't have to be overwhelming. By understanding how emotions influence decisions, communicating openly with professionals, and staying grounded in your goals, you turn what could be a stressful process into a fulfilling one.

Buying a home is more than a financial achievement; it is a milestone of stability, growth, and belonging. When approached with balance and patience, it becomes one of the most rewarding experiences in life.

Chapter 11

The Loan Officer's Challenges

The role of a loan officer carries both opportunity and responsibility. Mortgage professionals help people reach one of life's most meaningful milestones—homeownership. Along the way, they face demanding deadlines, complex regulations, detailed financial reviews, shifting market conditions, and emotional conversations with clients who may feel uncertain or overwhelmed.

To succeed, loan officers must combine technical knowledge with patience, integrity, and strong communication. True success is not measured only by the number of loans closed, but by the trust built, the guidance given, and the relationships maintained through dependable service.

Balancing Sales Goals with Ethics

Mortgage lending involves performance expectations. Most loan officers are expected to meet production goals, which can create healthy motivation but also significant pressure. The best professionals understand that ethical lending must always come first.

Every loan officer must balance several priorities:

- Meeting business goals
- Serving client needs responsibly
- Following compliance and legal standards
- Protecting personal and professional reputation

There will be times when a client qualifies for a loan that may not truly fit their budget or long-term plans. Ethical loan officers prioritize the borrower's wellbeing, even if it means delaying or declining the transaction. Protecting the client's financial health always outweighs short-term results. The most respected professionals build careers on honesty, not urgency.

Managing Multiple Clients and Deadlines

Loan officers often work with several clients at different stages of the process. Each client has unique needs, timelines, and financial circumstances. Staying organized is essential. A single missed document or miscommunication can delay a closing.

Strong organization includes:

- Tracking deadlines and rate lock expirations
- Reviewing and verifying borrower documents
- Coordinating with processors, underwriters, and title professionals.

- Keeping real estate agents informed
- Monitoring program updates and changing interest rates
- Providing proactive communication to clients

A well-organized loan officer creates confidence for both borrowers and colleagues. Clients appreciate clear updates and timely responses, and referral partners value reliability. Organization and communication are what transform a stressful process into a smooth one.

Handling Rejections and Difficult Conversations

Not every loan will be approved. Sometimes a borrower's credit history, income, or property details do not meet current requirements. These moments test a loan officer's professionalism and empathy.

The way a loan officer handles rejection often determines whether that client returns in the future. Rather than focusing on the denial, skilled professionals focus on education and solutions.

Professional loan officers:

- Explain the reasons for denial clearly and respectfully
- Offer specific steps to strengthen eligibility
- Encourage continued financial improvement
- Remain supportive and available for future guidance

Many borrowers who are not ready today become homeowners later because of honest advice and consistent encouragement from a patient loan officer.

Balancing Empathy with Compliance

Loan officers often hear about clients' personal stories, family goals, career changes, and financial setbacks. Empathy helps build trust and understanding, but every loan must still follow strict lending standards. The balance lies in showing compassion while staying compliant.

That balance looks like:

- Listening without judgment
- Treating every client with respect and patience
- Following underwriting and regulatory guidelines precisely
- Offering creative solutions within legal and ethical limits

Empathy without structure can create risk; compliance without compassion can create distance. The strongest professionals find a healthy balance between the two.

Staying Motivated in a Competitive Industry

Mortgage lending moves in cycles. There are busy times when rates are low and applications pour in, and there are slower seasons when persistence is essential. Market conditions, economic changes, and regulations constantly shift. Successful loan officers learn to adapt.

Motivation in this career grows from purpose. Each closed loan represents a milestone in someone's life. Seeing a client or family receive the keys to their home brings a satisfaction that numbers alone cannot provide.

Long-term success depends on:

- Continuous learning and product knowledge
- Consistency and time management
- Ethical commitment to every client
- Strong communication and empathy
- Building lasting relationships with clients and referral partners

Loan officers who focus on quality service rather than short-term gain develop reputations that sustain them through every market cycle.

Guidance for New and Aspiring Loan Officers

For those entering the industry, strong habits and values form the foundation for success. The mortgage business rewards professionalism, curiosity, and genuine care for people.

Key habits to develop early:

- Learn loan programs and eligibility rules thoroughly
- Communicate clearly, calmly, and confidently
- Stay organized with both digital and physical files
- Seek mentorship from experienced colleagues
- Treat every client with equal respect and attention
- Focus on education rather than pressure
- Protect your integrity at all costs

A loan officer's career grows through consistency and trust. Each satisfied borrower can become a lifelong advocate and source of referrals. The mortgage industry rewards those who serve with honesty, humility, and commitment to excellence.

The most effective loan officers are not just financial experts; they are educators, advisors, and advocates. Their work bridges technical skill with human understanding. By maintaining ethics, empathy, and organization, a loan officer becomes more than a professional; they become a trusted guide on one of life's most important journeys.

Chapter 12

Life After the Loan

Closing on a home is a major accomplishment, but the journey does not end when the papers are signed and the keys are handed over. Homeownership brings new responsibilities that go beyond making monthly payments. This next phase is about protecting your investment, maintaining financial discipline, and planning for long-term stability.

A successful homeowner is not just someone who buys responsibly, but someone who manages, maintains, and builds upon that decision. Loan officers also continue to play a role after closing. The best professionals remain available to their clients, offering education, guidance, and support as financial needs evolve.

Managing Your Mortgage After Purchase

Once the excitement of closing settles, the first priority is creating a consistent and reliable payment routine. Staying organized from the start prevents stress later and protects your credit standing.

Homeowners should:

- Review each monthly payment breakdown, including principal, interest, taxes, and insurance.
- Set up automatic payments to avoid missed due dates.
- Create digital or calendar reminders for each billing cycle.
- Monitor escrow account changes related to property taxes or insurance.

Regular payment habits keep your mortgage in good standing and establish the kind of credit history that opens future opportunities. Always review any notices or letters from your lender; these communications often include important updates about taxes, escrow adjustments, or servicing changes.

Avoiding Missed Payments and Financial Stress

Even with careful planning, life can bring unexpected financial challenges such as job changes, medical expenses, or temporary income loss. While these situations can be stressful, proactive communication with your lender is the best way to protect your finances.

Helpful strategies include:

- Maintaining an emergency fund equal to several months of expenses

- Learning about your lender's hardship or forbearance programs
- Contacting your loan servicer immediately if you expect payment difficulty
- Budgeting for home maintenance and unexpected repairs

Most lenders offer solutions for short-term financial setbacks. Reaching out before a payment is missed allows them to help, prevents damage to your credit, and avoids unnecessary stress.

Refinancing — When It Helps and When It Doesn't

At some point, homeowners may consider refinancing their mortgage. Refinancing replaces the current loan with a new one, often to improve terms, change the loan type, or access built-up equity.

Refinancing can make sense when:

- Interest rates have fallen, reducing the cost of borrowing
- You plan to stay in the home long enough to offset closing costs
- Your credit has improved since the original loan
- You want to switch from an adjustable-rate loan to a fixed rate
- Consolidating debts results in a lower overall payment.

However, refinancing may not be beneficial when:

- The upfront costs are higher than the potential savings
- You expect to sell or relocate in the near future
- Extending the loan term increases total interest paid
- The goal is short-term cash rather than long-term improvement

Before refinancing, calculate your "break-even point" — the time it takes for savings to outweigh costs. Discuss your options with a trusted loan professional who can help evaluate the long-term impact.

Maintaining Good Credit and Financial Health

Financial responsibility does not end after closing. Good credit remains essential for future borrowing, refinancing, or even insurance discounts. Maintaining healthy habits ensures ongoing financial flexibility.

Smart post-closing habits include:

- Paying all bills on time
- Avoiding unnecessary new debt
- Keeping credit card balances within reasonable limits
- Reviewing credit reports periodically to confirm accuracy

Homeownership strengthens financial discipline. By maintaining consistent credit habits, you create a foundation that supports future goals such as investment, business financing, or property upgrades.

Protecting and Improving the Property

Your home is both a place to live and a long-term financial asset. Regular maintenance and thoughtful improvements preserve its value and protect your investment.

Homeowners should plan for:

- Routine maintenance such as servicing HVAC systems and inspecting roofs
- Prompt repairs to prevent small issues from becoming expensive ones
- Seasonal care like cleaning gutters and maintaining landscaping
- Energy-efficient upgrades or thoughtful renovations when the budget allows

Caring for a home increases comfort, enhances value, and protects against unnecessary future costs. A well-maintained property also builds pride and confidence in ownership.

For Loan Officers — Turning Clients into Lifelong Relationships

The best loan officers know that the relationship does not end at closing. Continued support creates trust and long-term loyalty. Staying connected after the transaction turns one-time clients into lifelong advocates.

Effective post-closing practices include:

- Periodic check-ins or anniversary messages
- Offering guidance when market conditions change
- Sharing helpful articles or educational updates
- Providing honest advice about refinancing opportunities
- Staying available for questions long after the loan has closed

Consistent follow-up keeps the relationship personal and genuine. Clients remember professionals who continue to care after the sale. This kind of service builds both reputation and referral networks that last throughout a career.

Homeownership as a Path to Financial Growth

A mortgage is more than a monthly obligation. It is a tool that, when managed wisely, builds wealth and long-term stability. Each payment contributes to equity; an asset that grows over time and can support future financial goals.

Homeownership also brings a sense of belonging and community. It encourages responsibility, planning, and investment in the future. The true goal is not just to own a home, but to own it with confidence, understanding, and lasting financial health.

The journey to homeownership does not end at closing; it simply changes direction. Responsible payment habits, property care, and open communication with professionals keep your investment secure.

For homeowners, the reward is long-term stability. For loan officers, it is the satisfaction of seeing clients thrive long after the paperwork is complete. Homeownership is not the finish line; it is the foundation for financial growth and lifelong achievement.

Chapter 13

Building Financial Wisdom

A mortgage is only one part of a larger financial journey. Buying a home is a meaningful achievement, but staying financially strong after the purchase matters just as much. True success comes when homeownership fits within a broader plan for stability, growth, and generational progress.

Financial wisdom helps Homeowners protect what they've worked for and keep working towards their long-term goals. Whether someone is buying their first home or managing several properties, they need to keep learning and making smart financial decisions if they want to be successful in the long run.

Why Financial Literacy Matters for Homeowners

Financial literacy means understanding how money works; how to earn it, manage it, save it, and make informed choices about spending and investment. Homeownership adds new layers of responsibility, from mortgage payments to insurance, taxes, and maintenance. When homeowners understand these financial pieces, they gain control, reduce stress, and make confident decisions that protect their future.

Financial literacy strengthens long-term homeownership by:

- Managing monthly expenses effectively
- Preparing for emergencies and unexpected events
- Encouraging responsible credit habits
- Supporting smart decisions about refinancing or home improvements
- Building confidence in financial planning and investment

A strong grasp of financial principles transforms homeownership from a challenge into an opportunity for growth and peace of mind.

Creating a Sustainable Budget

Owning a home changes the way money flows each month. Beyond the mortgage, new costs arise that renters rarely face. A thoughtful budget keeps these obligations manageable and ensures that financial goals remain within reach.

A homeowner's budget should include:

- Mortgage payments
- Property taxes and homeowners' insurance
- Utilities and services
- Routine maintenance and seasonal upkeep
- Emergency repairs
- Long-term improvements or renovations

An effective budget doesn't just track expenses; it balances priorities. It leaves room for savings, future goals, and a little flexibility for life's surprises. A well-planned budget keeps homeownership enjoyable, sustainable, and free from unnecessary financial strain.

Building and Protecting Home Equity

Equity is the portion of your home that truly belongs to you. Each payment you make and each increase in property value helps that ownership grow. Over time, equity becomes one of the most powerful assets a household can build.

Equity can serve as a financial safety net or a foundation for future opportunities, such as:

- Refinancing for improved terms when appropriate
- Funding education, business, or retirement plans
- Purchasing investment property
- Building intergenerational wealth

You should be careful when using equity. Using home equity as an emergency fund or a way to spend money can hurt your long-term financial stability. The most successful homeowners see equity as a long-term, strategic tool that provides security and opportunity for decades, not just months.

Planning for Emergencies and Future Goals

Life brings both expected and unexpected changes. Responsible financial planning allows homeowners to face those changes with confidence. Setting aside an emergency fund; ideally covering three to six months of living expenses protects against temporary hardship such as job loss, medical costs, or sudden repairs.

Beyond short-term security, a homeowner's long-term financial plan may include:

- Saving for retirement
- Building college or education funds
- Planning for home upgrades or expansions
- Exploring property investments
- Supporting small business or community ventures

When a home is viewed as part of a complete financial picture, it becomes a stepping stone to broader success and stability.

Using Homeownership as a Wealth-Building Tool

Owning a home can be one of the best ways to build wealth, but only if you own it responsibly and consistently. Stable housing costs and rising property values create long-term financial benefits.

Smart homeowners build wealth by:

- Keeping housing costs stable compared to rising rents

- Letting equity grow naturally
- Making improvements that add value carefully and strategically
- Taking advantage of eligible tax benefits
- Keeping up with payments that help your credit score

The goal is not to see a home as a quick way to make money, but as a key part of long-term financial health. Homeownership can lead to independence and security for generations if you are patient and plan well.

Continuing Education and Professional Resources

The process of learning doesn't end. The housing and financial markets change, and homeowners who stay informed can make smart decisions. A big difference can be made by using reliable information sources and getting professional help.

Helpful resources include:

- Books and online courses on personal finance and budgeting
- HUD-approved housing counseling agencies
- Local and national homebuyer education workshops
- Government and nonprofit housing programs
- Certified financial planners or advisors
- Reputable industry publications and newsletters

Education builds confidence. The more a homeowner understands about money, credit, and planning, the easier it becomes to make choices that align with their goals.

Financial Wisdom That Lasts a Lifetime

Owning a home is more than just a milestone. It is the start of a long journey with finances. Homeowners can build a future that supports both their own stability and their family's legacy by being responsible with their money, saving steadily, and planning ahead.

The goal is not just to own a home, but to do well in it. You should be able to live comfortably, protect your investment, and get stronger with every financial decision you make. One of the best things about owning a home is the knowledge you gain along the way.

Chapter 14

The Future of Mortgage Lending

The mortgage business is always changing. Changes in technology, rules, and what customers want are all affecting how loans are processed and delivered. The purpose of lending is still the same: to assist people responsibly buy a home. However, the ways that this goal is reached are changing.

The financing climate now is speedier, more open, and more computerized. Borrowers want things to be easy, lenders want things to be quick, and both sides benefit from having more access to information. Despite all the new ideas, one thing will always be true: trust and human judgement will always be important. Technology can make the process better, but it can't take the place of talking to someone or getting expert help.

How Technology Is Reshaping the Mortgage Experience

Modern lending systems allow tasks that once took days to happen in minutes. Borrowers can now:

- Upload and sign documents securely online
- Track the progress of their loan in real time

- Receive instant updates through mobile apps or email
- Use automated systems to verify income, credit, and employment
- Complete much of the closing process electronically, where regulations allow

These tools save time and reduce errors. Lenders can review information more accurately, while borrowers gain transparency and convenience. When used correctly, technology creates a smoother experience for everyone involved.

However, digital tools still rely on accurate data and strong communication. Even the most advanced systems cannot make sense of missing or unclear information — that's where people remain essential.

The Rise of Online Lending and Automation

Online mortgage platforms are becoming a major part of the industry. Many use automation to analyze credit, verify assets, and estimate eligibility almost instantly. For straightforward applications, this can greatly reduce waiting time and speed up approvals.

Automation helps by:

- Identifying potential issues early in the process
- Simplifying document submission
- Offering instant rate comparisons

- Allowing borrowers to explore options at their own pace

Still, every borrower's story is unique. Automated systems can process numbers, but they cannot fully evaluate complex income situations, self-employment, or the nuances of personal goals. That is why experienced loan officers remain invaluable; they interpret the data, explain options, and help borrowers make choices that align with long-term financial comfort.

The Growth of Instant Approvals and Digital Closings

For borrowers with clear financial histories and strong credit, some lenders now offer near-instant approval decisions. Digital closing technology has also expanded, allowing buyers to sign key documents remotely when permitted by state law.

These advancements simplify logistics and fit the pace of modern life. Yet not every transaction fits the automated mold. Unique income sources, special property types, or complex financial structures often require manual review. Technology offers speed, but accuracy and careful validation will always define responsible lending.

Why Human Insight Still Matters

Even in a digital world, buying a home remains an emotional and deeply personal milestone. Borrowers experience excitement, uncertainty, and hope; feelings that no algorithm can address.

Loan officers provide the human balance technology cannot. They:

- Listen carefully and translate complex terms into plain language
- Guide borrowers through difficult moments
- Resolve issues that automation cannot anticipate
- Offer reassurance and context when decisions feel overwhelming
- Advocate for clients when clarification or flexibility is needed

Technology processes data; people provide understanding. The best mortgage experience combines both efficient systems supported by empathetic professionals.

The Evolving Role of the Modern Loan Officer

The loan officer's role is shifting from paperwork manager to trusted financial advisor. Modern professionals use technology to handle routine tasks so they can focus more on personalized service.

Their effectiveness now depends on how well they integrate innovation with human connection.

A forward-thinking loan officer:

- Stays current with industry regulations and digital tools
- Understands both traditional and online lending systems
- Guides borrowers through technology with patience and clarity
- Maintains transparency and ethics in every transaction
- Balances efficiency with care, ensuring clients never feel reduced to a number

This combination of technical skill and human empathy defines the next generation of lending excellence.

Preparing for the Mortgage Landscape Ahead

The future of mortgage lending will continue to evolve around three main goals: speed, clarity, and fairness. Both borrowers and professionals can prepare by committing to continuous learning. Staying informed about market shifts, lending policies, and financial trends ensures decisions remain sound and responsible.

Key areas to watch include:

- Updates to federal and state lending laws
- Advances in digital verification and closing platforms
- Emerging credit models and affordability programs
- Shifts in housing market demand and economic cycles

While systems and technology will keep improving, the foundation of good lending remains unchanged: honesty, diligence, clear communication, and respect for the borrower's long-term well-being.

The Balance Between Innovation and Integrity

While technology advances society, integrity builds trust. Those who embrace both will have the most successful future in mortgage lending, leveraging innovation to streamline the process while maintaining the human touch that characterizes excellent service.

One tenet will endure as the sector develops and changes: every loan represents a person, a family, and a home-buying dream. Homeownership will always be fundamentally human, even as lending becomes more digital.

Chapter 15

Final Reflections — More Than a Loan

The mortgage process involves more than just money. It molds long-term opportunity, stability, and confidence. For purchasers, it is the start of a new chapter, one that is full of endeavor, hope, and personal development. It stands for a pledge made by loan officers to treat people with integrity, tolerance, and consideration.

Being a homeowner involves more than just getting keys and signing paperwork. It's about getting ready, learning, and laying the groundwork for the future. A mortgage is a partnership based on mutual respect and trust, not just a transaction.

Life is in motion for those who work in the mortgage industry. Every client has different objectives, queries, and difficulties. Every story serves as a reminder that lending is about more than just numbers; it's also about advice, instruction, and interpersonal relationships. Listening, providing clear explanations, and showing respect for each client are frequently the most important lessons learnt.

Confidence increases on both sides when communication is consistent and information is clear.

Everyone gains from a careful approach: the professional gains credibility through honesty and reliability, and the buyer feels understood.

Why Integrity, Education, and Empathy Matter

Integrity protects both the borrower and the lender. It ensures that decisions are honest, fair, and built on respect. Education empowers clients to make choices that fit their goals and long-term comfort. Empathy gives professionals the ability to listen, understand, and guide without judgment.

When these three qualities work together, lending transforms from being just a business to a meaningful service. Every loan represents a story: a family finding their first home, an individual rebuilding stability, or a couple planning for the future. Loan officers who understand this never take the responsibility lightly. They explain, guide, and reassure, knowing that the impact of their work can last for years.

Encouragement for Homebuyers

Homeownership is a journey, not a race. It takes patience, preparation, and steady progress. Move at a pace that supports your comfort and stability. Ask questions freely. Compare your options carefully.

Focus on the long-term picture rather than short-term excitement or outside pressure.

The perfect home complements both your way of life and your peace of mind. Instead of causing stress, it should increase security. Homeownership is one of the most fulfilling investments you can make in your life if you approach it patiently and clearly. It's a place where future plans are shaped and memories are created.

Keep in mind that preparation gives you control and knowledge gives you confidence. The process goes more smoothly when you understand it.

A Message to Loan Officers

Every mortgage application is more than paperwork; it represents trust. Each file is someone's story, often tied to years of hard work and hope. Treat it with care.

Lead with clarity. Explain every step in a way that empowers your clients. When challenges arise, approach them calmly and look for solutions. Respect every client's pace, background, and goals.

Lasting success in this profession does not come from closing the most loans, but from closing them responsibly. When you prioritize service over sales, clients remember your integrity. They return, they refer, and they build your reputation for years to come.

A strong loan officer builds not just transactions but relationships. By focusing on people first, you become a trusted guide in one of the most important decisions of their lives.

Conclusion

The mortgage process is not a single event. It is a path built from many steps; preparation, review, communication, and steady decision-making. Success depends on understanding each stage and staying focused on long-term goals.

For buyers, the message is simple: prepare early, ask questions, and make choices that align with your comfort and future. Homeownership should strengthen your financial life and bring peace of mind, not pressure.

For mortgage professionals, the journey is a commitment to service. Guiding clients with honesty, patience, and expertise builds both professional pride and community trust.

The mortgage journey, at its heart, is about partnership between knowledge and action, between buyers and lenders, between dreams and reality. When approached with care, clarity, and integrity, it becomes more than a financial milestone. It becomes a foundation for stability, growth, and a better future.

Bonus Resources

These resources support both homebuyers and mortgage professionals. They are designed to provide structure, clarity and preparation for each step of the mortgage journey.

Mortgage Readiness Checklist for Homebuyers

Use this checklist before starting the mortgage process to ensure a strong foundation.

Financial Preparation

- ☐ Stable employment and consistent income
- ☐ Emergency savings for unexpected expenses
- ☐ Reviewed personal budget and comfortable payment range
- ☐ No recent late payments on credit accounts
- ☐ Plan for down payment and closing costs
- ☐ Understanding of monthly mortgage expenses including taxes and insurance

Credit and Documentation

- ☐ Checked credit report for accuracy
- ☐ Reduced credit card balances when possible
- ☐ Avoided new loans or credit applications
- ☐ Organized recent pay stubs and bank statements
- ☐ Gathered tax returns and identification documents

Home Search Preparation

☐ Received pre-approval from a trusted lender
☐ Clear idea of desired location and property type
☐ Worked with a real estate professional if needed
☐ Reviewed responsibilities of homeownership
☐ Set expectations for timing and process

Being prepared brings confidence, clarity and a smoother experience.

Communication Templates for Loan Officers

These templates support professional and clear communication with clients.

Initial Introduction

Thank you for reaching out. I look forward to assisting you with your home financing goals. To begin, we will review your financial information, discuss loan options and help determine the best path for your home purchase. Please have your recent pay stubs, bank statements and identification available so we can get started confidently. I am here to guide you through every step.

Document Request

To move forward, we need the following documents. Providing them promptly helps keep the process on schedule. If you have questions or need help locating anything, please let me know. We are here to support you.

Pre-Approval Completion

Your pre-approval is complete. This prepares you to begin the home search confidently and shows sellers that you are a qualified buyer. Your next steps are to work with your real estate professional, stay in communication and notify me of any changes to your financial situation.

Pre-Closing Reminder

As we approach closing, please avoid major financial changes. Do not open new credit, change jobs or make large purchases unless we discuss it beforehand. These steps protect your loan approval and ensure a smooth closing experience.

Clear communication helps clients stay calm, prepared and informed.

First-Time Homebuyer Program and Grant List in the United States

These resources support eligible buyers seeking financial assistance or favorable loan terms. Programs change, so checking current eligibility and availability is important.

Federal Programs

- FHA loans
- VA loans for eligible military members and spouses
- USDA loans for qualifying rural and suburban areas
- Down payment assistance programs dependent on location
- Good Neighbor Next Door program for public service professionals

State and Local Options

Most states offer first-time buyer grants, down payment assistance or low-interest programs through local housing agencies. Many cities and counties also provide support programs based on income and property location.

Where to Check

- State housing finance agencies
- Local housing departments
- HUD program directories
- Community lending programs through banks and credit unions

These programs help remove barriers and create opportunities for responsible, prepared buyers.

Glossary of Mortgage Terms

A simple reference to common terms used throughout the mortgage process.

Appraisal
A professional estimate of a home's market value.

Closing Disclosure
A final summary of loan terms, payments and closing costs provided before signing.

Debt-to-Income Ratio
The percentage of monthly income used to pay debt obligations.

Equity
The portion of the property owned by the homeowner after subtracting the loan balance.

Escrow
An account used to hold funds for taxes and insurance paid as part of the mortgage payment.

Interest Rate
The cost of borrowing money for the loan, expressed as a percentage.

Pre-Approval
Verification of a borrower's financial readiness to purchase a home.

Principal
The portion of the mortgage payment that reduces the loan balance.

References

Consumer Financial Protection Bureau (CFPB).
"Your Home Loan Toolkit: A Step-by-Step Guide."
Washington, DC: U.S. Government Printing Office, 2024.
https://www.consumerfinance.gov

Federal Housing Administration (FHA).
"Single Family Housing Policy Handbook (HUD 4000.1)."
U.S. Department of Housing and Urban Development, 2023.
https://www.hud.gov/program_offices/housing/fhahandbook

Fannie Mae.
"Understanding the Mortgage Process."
Federal National Mortgage Association, 2023.
https://www.fanniemae.com

Experian.
Axelton, Karen. *"How Does Your Credit Score Affect Your Interest Rate?"*
Experian Consumer Services, September 26, 2023.
https://www.experian.com

Freddie Mac.
"CreditSmart® Homebuyer U."

Federal Home Loan Mortgage Corporation, 2024.
https://www.freddiemac.com/creditsmart

Made in the USA
Coppell, TX
19 February 2026

71825956R00069